God is REAL

Praise

"This book is a good reminder for us not to let all the fuss in the day take us away from the many blessings we have in our daily lives." — Martha

"It's been a hectic month with family, community, work, school and all the goings on in our world. I needed a reminder to slow down and embrace the journey." — Elizabeth

"Your art work is phenomenal; the stories are inspirational; and the story about Natalie has encouraged me to reach out to someone who has been on my mind. What a treasure." — John

"Thank you for making this book become a book for me. I'm thankful to know that God is real in my life, too." — Adam

This book belongs to:

_____

Cover and interior design by Liz Riviere

God is REAL

Copyright © 2021 by Ssusan Forte O'Neill (art and text)
Published by Ace Diversified Services, Inc.

To learn more about Ssusan Forte O'Neill, visit fortedesignstoo.net.

ISBN: 978-0-9790729-6-3
Library of Congress Control Number: 2021913854

Printed by Minuteman Press, Dana Point, CA

Printed in the United States of America

Made with loving hearts in the United States of America

God

is

REAL

An Invitation to
Access and Embrace God
in Your Daily Life

SSUSAN FORTE O'NEILL

Dedication

To Our Heavenly Father,
for His Everlasting Love

To my loving husband,
with whom I'm blessed to walk hand-in hand in life,
for his patience and encouragement
that inspire me every day to live a life of joy through all seasons

To Sue, my long-time friend and prayer partner,
for her compassionate heart

To Liz, my friend and colleague,
for her peaceful approach and dedicated creative collaboration
that transform my visions and dreams into an illustrated voice

To the Circle of Love Ladies,
Bev, Faye, Heather, Maria and Patricia,
who bless me with their sacred sharing and joyous hearts

To Ed, my publisher and friend,
for his kindness and belief in my creative endeavors
and for always responding with "why not?" to all of my ideas

Start your journey...

Invitation

If you are reading this book, you may already know that God is REAL,
but perhaps you are questioning if He hears your prayers and knows your heart.
Well, yes, He does. You are a beautiful child of God.
You are here today as He created you with His love. He loves you.
He knows everything about you. You are a miracle.
You are a reflection of God that is real.

May these every day encounters with God that were told to me
inspire you to live a life fulfilled with His love and promises.
May they encourage you to believe in God's love.

Invite God into your heart, as your Heavenly Father
and allow him to plant His love in your garden of life.
Walk with him, hand-in-hand,
and live a life of joy through all seasons.

"…with God all things are possible." Matthew 19:26 (NIV)

Trust

Trust in the Lord with all your heart
and lean not on your own understanding;
in all your ways submit to him,
and he will make your paths straight.

Proverbs 3:5-6 (NIV)

Trust

The Lord alone is our radiant hope and we trust in him with all our hearts.
His wrap-around presence will strengthen us.

Psalm 33:20 (TPT)

We met Miguel on a road trip through central California. At a very young age, Miguel left his home in Yucatan, Mexico to come to America. He landed in San Francisco and, since he did not know the English language at the time, his first job was as a dishwasher at a restaurant.

A few years later, he was taken under the wing of Michel, a chef who mentored and trained him in the classical French tradition. At his restaurant, he creates a cuisine that celebrates rigorously sourced local and sustainable ingredients infused with the vibrant regional flavors of his homeland and the classical French finesse of his training. Miguel introduced us to his "home" of new flavors. And when we had finished dining, Miguel came to sit with us at our table. He announced the closing of his restaurant due to escalating rent.

Miguel's Story

There are always ups and downs, but God has always been in my creative heart guiding me on His journey. Through the valleys and mountains of life, He is always with me and I know it's all going to work out.

You see, in life, we all have ups and downs, but when you believe in God, He will always show you the way. He has for me my whole life. I have been able to follow my creative heart and live a life beyond my imagination and have been very blessed with a wonderful family.

If we allow our Heavenly Father to be the cornerstone of our hearts and we set out to build a beautiful home of love wherever we may be, home is where the heart is. God's desire is for us to be filled with His loving blessings and beauty—this is His home for us through all seasons of life.

When one door closes, open a door to God. I know it is an old cliché, yet when we open our hearts to put our trust in God, he always opens a door for us beyond our imagination—if we choose to believe.

"You will seek me and find me when you seek me with all your heart. I will be found by you," declares the Lord...

Jeremiah 29:13-14 (NIV)

Trust LESSON

And we know that in all things God works for the good of those who love him,
who have been called according to his purpose.   Romans 8:28 (NIV)

Our Heavenly Father is knocking at the door of your heart, hoping you'll open
it to his loving kindness and blessings. Do you hear His knock on your heart?
Open the door, and you will be richly surprised with the many promises and
blessings He has in store for you. Write down the desires of your heart,
meditate and pray upon them. Wait to hear God's voice through His word
to see where He guides you.

_____

_____

_____

_____

_____

_____

_____

Faith

For I am the Lord your God
who takes hold of your right hand
and says to you, Do not fear;
I will help you.

Isaiah 41:13 (NIV)

Faith

Blessed is the man who trusts in the Lord,
And whose trust is the Lord.
For he will be like a tree planted by the water
That extends its roots by a stream,
And does not fear when the heat comes;
But its leaves will be green,
And it will not be anxious in a year of drought

Jeremiah 17:7 (NASB)

On a recent trip to Tanzania, my husband and I were reminded that God's blessings come in all different shapes and sizes. One night, Jonathan, our guide, asked if he could talk with us for a little while to share a story with us about a miracle from God. We sat outside by the fire with a blanket of stars putting on a spectacular light show.

Jonathan's Story

Fifteen months ago, I was in a severe car accident. I was driving and it was a rainy evening. The roads were not paved. There were no lights.

Suddenly, a large truck ran into my car. I was thrown out of the car and landed on the field next to the road. This is what I was told -- I do not remember all that happened.

I arrived at the hospital with a very badly broken leg. The doctors told me that they were not sure if they could save my leg, and if they could, they were not sure that I would be able to walk normally again.

I would pray and commune with God throughout the day which gave me such peace as I was healing. I also prayed that my wife and child would be at peace. I gave thanks for all the blessings in my life. The surgery took many hours followed by several weeks of recovery. I made prayer my focus, twice a day.

The doctors were not sure if I would ever walk again but, as you can see, I am able to run. I am able to run and play with my daughter who was born just a few months after I was released from the hospital. You see I know God is real, He answered my prayers and my family's prayers and I am here with you to share our beautiful country.

Faith LESSON

Jonathan's faith is deeply rooted. We are reminded that we have nothing to be anxious about or fear if we put our trust and faith in God.

When was the last time you took a sip of water, felt a raindrop on your hand, or took a deep breath of fresh air? When was the last time you gave thanks for the gifted resources of life -- the breathe you take, the water you drink, the food you eat, the family and friends you have?

Make a list of things you have to be thankful for. Watch how quickly your list overflows the page. Have the courage to walk in Faith and discover the many blessings He has promised for you.

_____

_____

_____

_____

_____

_____

Share God's love
through the gift of

Kindness

Kindness

…Your tender care and kindness leave no one forgotten,
not a man or even a mouse. Psalm 36:6 (TPT)

Although most of the area was enveloped in heavy fog on the day we arrived, the small town of Skagway, Alaska boasted clear weather and comfortable temperatures. As we walked around the town, we discovered a quaint shop with unique handmade treasures and carpets. The husband and wife owners, Anthony and Elizabeth, spent hours with us, telling us about their life journeys, how they met and what brought them to Skagway. Anthony shared some of his favorite Turkish tea made in his hometown and, when we parted, we left with the gift of a new friendship and some treasures from their store. They told us that they would be visiting the area where we live in a few months and we told them we couldn't wait to return their kindness and hospitality.

A few months later, Anthony and Elizabeth scheduled time to join us at our home and, during their visit, shared exciting news. They had just learned that they were expecting their first child. As we celebrated, I gave them a small angel I had made of yarn to accompany them home.

A year later, our neighbors Wally and Mary shared that they would be traveling to Alaska and we urged them to stop in Skagway to visit our friends Anthony and Elizabeth. One afternoon I received a call from Mary who had just arrived home from Alaska. "I have an amazing story to share with you. I promised Anthony and Elizabeth that calling you would be the first thing I did when I got home."

Mary's Story

Elizabeth delivered the baby in the next town over, at a small medical center. During the delivery, there were complications that caused life-threatening medical issues for the baby. They rushed the baby to Anchorage via helicopter to a major medical hospital to try to save the baby's life.

Time was precious and they could only take the baby in the helicopter. As the nurses and doctors rushed the baby to the heliport, Elizabeth tucked the angel you gave them in next to their baby.

She remembered the prayers you shared and repeated them as the helicopter whisked their baby away. Anthony and Elizabeth told me that after they prayed, they both felt a warmth of comfort come over them. They said that although they did not really know about God, at that very moment, they both knew that God was REAL as they could feel a swell of peace.

The baby made it to the hospital just in time to be met by a crew of doctors and nurses. Anthony and Elizabeth were able to get transportation to the hospital the next day to be with their baby and, as mother and baby recovered, they were finally able to be with their beautiful, healthy baby girl. They set up a little nursery in the shop's office and guess what's perched on a shelf in the office? The angel! Your angel! Elizabeth said that she tells her daughter the story of the angel every night. It's her daughter's favorite.

Kindness LESSON

Be inspired to share the gift of kindness with others and embrace a journey filled with love and blessings from our Heavenly Father.

When was the last time you did something kind for a family member, friend or stranger? When was the last time you said hello to a neighbor, gave a hand to someone in need or sent a note with some words of encouragement to a parent, sister, brother or friend?

_____

_____

_____

_____

_____

_____

_____

Prayer

Then you will call on me
and come and pray to me,
and I will listen to you.

Jeremiah 29:12 (NIV)

Prayer

We all experience times of testing which is normal for every human being.
But God will be faithful to you. He will screen and filter the severity, nature,
and timing of every test or trial you face so that you can bear it.
And each test is an opportunity to trust him more,
for along with every trial God has provided for you a way of escape
that will bring you out of it victoriously.

1 Corinthians 10:13 (TPT)

The other day, we scheduled some repair work on our garage door. We were given a window of time for the technician's arrival but, on our day of service, that window was coming to a close, and we had not yet seen the technician.

I dialed customer service to check on the status of the technician and, while I was on hold, the doorbell rang.

I opened the door and was greeted by a bright smile.

"Hi, my name is Eddie. I am here to fix your garage door."

As we went out to the garage, I told Eddie how happy I was to see him. I praised God that he had arrived safely. Upon hearing my words, Eddie turned around and said, "I know God's love and I know God is real. I have seen his miracles – real miracles."

Eddie's Story

My wife and I were expecting a baby so we went to a have a routine check-up. As the doctor reviewed the sonogram, he announced that there were major problems with our baby and that we should consider aborting the child.

We were speechless. When we arrived home, I said to my wife, "Let's pray. We need to pray to God for his guidance."

I was not a believer at that time, but during this hour of need, I made a promise to God. I said, "God, if you are real, if you are really REAL, I give you my word. If you save my baby, I will dedicate my life to you and serve you for all my remaining days."

Weeks went by and at every doctor's appointment we were encouraged to abort the baby. But I told my wife that we could not give up. "We are going to keep praying and have faith in God's miracle promises."

Then the time to deliver the baby came. We went to the hospital together, in prayer, for the health of our child.

See the size of this garage? This was the size of the delivery room. It was filled with doctors and nurses, ready to take the baby away for emergency surgery. When the time came, and it was truly God's timing, our son was born and, to the total astonishment of all the doctors and nurses in the room, he was born healthy! We couldn't stop wiping away the tears of joy from our eyes. We had a healthy baby boy from God, Our God, the greatest miracle worker.

So, I am sorry if I was running a little late today. My wife, who is at home with our second son, asked me to take our first son to school. He is now five years old and, as you can understand, I could not miss the opportunity to spend a little extra time with him today.

I have kept my promise to God. In order to serve Him, I knew that I had to begin by understanding the Word of God. For the past five years, I have dedicated myself to learning the word and sharing the truth with others everywhere I walk.

I want to share with you one of my favorite bible verses that I have memorized so that it stays close to my heart and in my mind as a guide through any challenges I may face throughout the day.

My son, pay attention to what I say; turn your ear to my words.
Do not let them out of your sight, keep them within your heart;
for they are life to those who find them
and health to one's whole body.

Proverbs 4:20-22 (NIV)

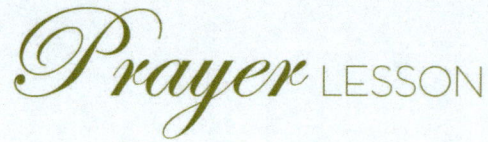Prayer LESSON

I would like to encourage you to enjoy your time with our Heavenly Father through the gift of prayer and fellowship. Prayer comes in many different forms from quiet alone times, worship and praise to small groups, ongoing conversations and communing with our Heavenly Father throughout the day.

Are you facing a challenge in your life? Do you wonder if God will hear your prayer? He does for God is REAL. Write down the troubles on your heart. Lean on God's word to guide you in prayer. Listen for God. Trust and see where He will guide you.

_____

_____

_____

_____

_____

_____

_____

Hope

*Let God's love fill you
with everlasting hope
for today and tomorrow.*

Hope

… those who hope in the Lord will renew their strength.
They will soar on wings like eagles; they will run and not grow weary,
they will walk and not be faint.   Isaiah 40:31 (NIV)

"Hope" in the New Testament is the Greek "elpis" or "elpizo" meaning a confident expectation or assurance based upon a sure foundation for which we wait with joy. In other words, "there is no doubt about it."

"Picture the word as you spell it; the big 'O' is an opening. For some it is an empty feeling or expression as though to throw a desire or dream to the open wind. And for others with a biblical perspective, it is an opening to stand with confidence in front of the endless opportunities that lie ahead, promised by our Heavenly Father," explained my friend Xzandrya.

Whether we realize it or not, we are woven together through all seasons. With hope, we have the courage to move forward in our lives.

Sarah is one of my dearest friends from elementary school and although we live in different parts of the country, we made a pact and met up on her birthday. Our friendship runs deep. There was a lot of hugging and rejoicing and then, all of a sudden, she sat back in her chair and her eyes began to water. Tears pooled then gently washed down her face. In her soft voice, she said that she had a story she needed to share with me. I didn't know what to think.

Sarah's Story

When I developed a training program a couple of years ago for an out-of-state client, the company assigned a point person named Natalie. I'd fly out every two weeks to discuss the direction of the program and eventually, Natalie and I became really good friends. We would talk about books, share recipes, and talk about our families. She would tell me stories about her early years growing up in Croatia and how she dreamed to go back and visit family and friends.

After about a year of working together, we were out for lunch and she announced to me that she has been fighting cancer for several years and that it was now in remission. She said she didn't want to burden anyone, that she was just trying to keep up with daily activities as much as possible, especially spending time with her son. Then she told me that she just found out that her father was in the early stages of Alzheimer's.

I was stunned because I had no idea. I asked her, "How have you gotten through these challenges? Where do you turn for hope?"

She looked at me and said, "I am not sure what you mean by hope. I trust my doctors but I don't believe in God."

Driving home after our luncheon, it hit me. I kept thinking about how, years ago, God had put on my heart to pray for "Natalie". That evening, I looked through my older journals and there, penned on the pages and in the margins, was "Pray for Natalie." That was twelve years ago. I didn't know anyone by the name of Natalie. I remember asking God, "Who is Natalie?" And every time I asked this question, I heard the same response: "Keep praying for Natalie."

And so I did.

When I first met Natalie, I didn't put two and two together that his may be "the Natalie". It wasn't until she told me that she has been battling cancer that I knew this had to be her.

It is almost too powerful for words, right? What a strong reminder that we may never know what God has planned for us, but if and when we truly trust Him with faith and love, He will show us His purpose.

Over the next several days, I thought and prayed. Do I tell Natalie that I believe she is the Natalie that God had prepared me to pray for these last twelve years? One night I was awakened by a quiet voice from God: "You will have a chance to tell her. She will need to hear that through your sharing of prayers, she was never alone."

When we met a week later, Natalie asked if we could sit outside, so we found a nice table under the shade of a tree. She talked about the ups and downs of her father's health and I felt a nudge from God, His voice was clear: "It's time to let her know I am REAL. I am the God that will give her hope."

When she finished sharing her father's updates, I took a deep breathe and said, 'Natalie, I know you have told me you don't believe in God, but I need to share this with you.'

'Twelve years ago, God put on my heart to pray for a Natalie but I didn't know anyone by the name of Natalie.' She looked at me a little bewildered.

I told her that when we had lunch last week and she told me the story about her health, I realized that she was the one that God had me pray for. "I have been praying for you, for twelve years," I said. "I believe God wanted you to know that you are not alone and He is with you. He wants you to have Hope."

At that moment, a soft cool breeze gently washed through the tree, like a comforting blanket from God.

Natalie sat very still, then looked at me with a sweet smile and said, "wow" and that she was thankful to know that someone was praying for her.

I said to her, "You are 'My Natalie' and I will continue to pray for you."

Even though our project is complete, we have kept in touch via email. And every time we email, she signs off with "Your Natalie".

Last Friday evening, I got a call from Natalie, which was unusual. She told me her father had passed away and she was unable to be with him during the last few days of life.

She quietly said, "Will you pray with me?"After she took a deep breath, she continued with a tearful voice and said, "I'm ready to open my heart to God to understand the hope you had talked about that He has for my life, too."

We spent several tearful moments praying together for God's love to fill her with peace and hope for an everlasting life.

Before we said our goodbyes, I told her, "Always know that you are never alone. Our God is there for us. He has you and your father etched on his heart for eternity."

And I shared one of my favorite bible verses from The Message Translation from Chapter 15 of the book of Romans that talks about God's promises and hope for all:

Oh! May the God of green hope fill you up with joy, fill you up with peace, so that your believing lives, filled with the life-giving energy of the Holy Spirit, will brim over with hope!

Romans 15:13 (The Message)

 *Hope* LESSON

It is always so fascinating to see how God reveals himself to us through other people.
Has God put a person on your mind or heart recently? Did you ignore God's voice or did you choose to walk with God and pray for guidance for why this person's name was put on your heart?

_____

_____

_____

_____

_____

_____

_____

_____

But those who wait on the Lord shall renew their strength;
they shall mount up with wings like eagles,
they shall run and not be weary, they shall walk and not faint.

Isaiah 40:31 (NKJV)

I encourage you to continue your journey
to discover how God is REAL in your life.
Take time to praise God for his love endures forever.
Let God's love fill your heart with thanksgiving and joy through all seasons.

Give thanks to the only miracle-working God!
His tender love for us continues on forever!
Give thanks to the Creator who made the heavens with wisdom!
His tender love for us continues on forever!
To him who formed dry ground, raising it up from the sea!
His tender love for us continues on forever!
Praise the one who created every heavenly light!
His tender love for us continues on forever!
He set the sun in the sky to rule over day!
His tender love for us continues on forever!
Praise him who set in place the moon
and stars to rule over the night!

Psalm 136: 4-9 (TPT)

JOURNEY NOTES

Dream   Pray   Believe

About the Author

Ssusan Forte O'Neill learned early on that the "gift of the heart" would be her treasured compassion of life to share with others. Throughout her journey as an artist, author, teacher and business visionary, she has chosen to express the mission of the "giving heart."

Ms. Forte O'Neill began her career by launching several small businesses, and is President and Founder of Forte Designs, a dedicated business development consultancy. She is also the Founder of the Technolink Association, a trade association and resource center for emerging and start-up companies, enhancing the development of innovation with public and private partnerships between universities and institutions of Southern California.

Trained in Fine Arts at George Washington University, Ms. Forte O'Neill works in various mediums from large-scale paintings and sumi style pen and ink to fiber and fabric. She compliments her artistry with a love for the written word and has authored *A Journey to Rediscover Your Heart* and *The Book of Herman.*

Ms. Forte O'Neill, when not on one of their travel adventures, resides in Southern California with her husband. She fills her days with inspiration from her garden, walking with nature, cooking, sharing in conversations with family and friends and exploring new paths of creativity.

For more inspiration, visit fortedesignstoo.net.

Made in the USA
Monee, IL
24 May 2023

34238934R00029